STOP OVERPAYING TAXES IN INDIA

7 LEGAL STRATEGIES TO MAXIMIZE PROFITS & SLASH COSTS FOR FOREIGN BUSINESS OWNERS

STOP OVERPAYING TAXES IN INDIA

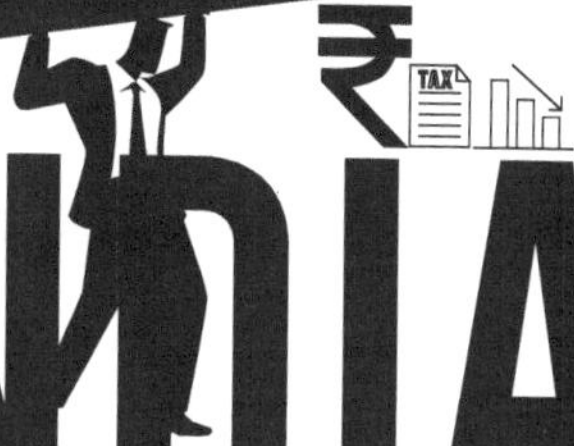

7 LEGAL STRATEGIES TO MAXIMIZE PROFITS & SLASH COSTS FOR FOREIGN BUSINESS OWNERS

CA MANISH GUPTA

Worldwide Published by

Pendown Press
PREMIUM BUSINESS PUBLISHER

PENDOWN PRESS LLP

An ISO 9001 & ISO 14001 Certified Co.,

Regd. Office: 3767A, Kanhaiya Nagar,

Tri Nagar, Delhi-110035

Ph.: 8130886000, 9650072927

E-mail: info@pendownpress.com

Branch Office: 1A/2A, 20, Hari Sadan, Ansari Road,

Daryaganj, New Delhi-110002

Ph.: 011-45794768

Website: PendownPress.com

Edition: 2025

Price: ₹ 399

ISBN: 978-93-6338-387-6

Layout and Cover Designed by Pendown Graphics Team

Dedicated to every entrepreneur who took the leap to enter India without a map, but with belief.

Your challenges became my chapters. Your trust became this book.

This is for you.

TABLE OF CONTENTS

TABLE OF CONTENTS

Disclaimer

The case studies and examples included in this book are provided for educational and illustrative purposes only. To protect client confidentiality and comply with non-disclosure agreements, all names, companies, and identifying details have been changed or anonymized.

The information, strategies, and insights presented are general in nature and should not be considered legal, financial, or professional advice. They are not a substitute for advice tailored to your specific situation.

Readers are encouraged to consult with qualified professionals or contact us directly before applying any strategies or making decisions based on this book.

Neither the authors, publishers, nor any associated parties can be held responsible for any loss, damage, or consequences resulting from the use of the information provided.

DISCLAIMER

ACKNOWLEDGEMENTS

This second book is a testament to the power of collaboration, resilience, and a shared vision. I am deeply grateful for the opportunity to share my insights with you, and I hope these pages inspire and empower you as much as my supporters have inspired me.

To my late father, Mr. Anil Gupta, your wisdom continues to light my path. To my mother, Mrs. Pushpa, your boundless love is my anchor. My wife, Disha, your unwavering support and patience made this journey possible. To my daughter, Vanya, your laughter fuels my purpose and reminds me to dream big.

I owe immense gratitude to my mentor, Mr. Akshar Yadav, who taught me the art of crafting a book with clarity and heart. Your guidance was my compass.

To my Board of Directors, thank you for your dedication to ensuring this book was completed on time, with a mission to empower foreign business owners. Your vision elevated this work.

To my MAG team members, your candid feedback and teamwork shaped this book into something truly special. Your contributions are woven into every chapter.

To Himanshu, my partner and greatest ally, this book would not exist without you. Your support at every step—from ideation to completion—made all the difference.

To Dinesh Verma and the Pendown Press team, thank you for your expertise and commitment to bringing this book to the world.

And to you, my readers, thank you for choosing to engage with my work. Your trust and time inspire me to keep creating.

To all named and those whose quiet support touched this project, thank you for being part of this milestone. Together, we've built something meaningful, and I'm excited for what lies ahead.

With heartfelt gratitude,

CA Manish Gupta

❑ ❑ ❑

PREFACE

When I wrote my first book, Hassle-Free Business Setup in India, I was overwhelmed by stories from foreign entrepreneurs who found clarity in navigating India's complex business landscape. Their journeys, filled with courage and determination, inspired me deeply. Yet, one challenge kept emerging: taxes. Time and again, I saw business owners—founders, finance heads, and legal teams—lose lakhs of dollars annually due to avoidable tax mistakes. These weren't due to a lack of effort but rather a lack of guidance, timely information and clear understanding. As a consultant, I've helped over 300 foreign businesses overcome these hurdles through practical advice and hands-on support. But my time is limited, and I can't be everywhere at once.

This realization sparked a mission: to share simple, ethical, and actionable tax-saving strategies with every foreign business owner striving to succeed in India. I wanted to create something lasting, something that could travel beyond boardrooms and consulting calls, and reach those who need it most.

Stop Overpaying Taxes in India is the culmination of that mission. This book distills my experience into seven practical strategies designed to help you boost profits without getting lost in technical jargon or fearing notices from tax authorities. These are not tax-escaping mechanisms but transparent, implementable approaches that respect India's laws while maximizing your financial potential. Whether you're setting up a new venture or scaling an existing company, this book is your guide to making informed and confident tax decisions. Each chapter is designed to give you clarity, reduce risk and increase peace of mind, so you can focus on growing your business instead of worrying about compliance.

India's economic rise is drawing global entrepreneurs, but its tax complexities can be daunting. My goal is to empower you with knowledge that feels like a conversation with a trusted mentor—clear, direct, and focused on your success. The stories of clients who transformed their businesses by applying these strategies continue to inspire me every day, and I believe you can achieve the same.

I invite you to dive into these pages, explore the strategies, and discuss them with your team. Don't just read; take notes, ask questions, and reflect on how each insight applies to your unique business context. Implement these tips, and you'll not only save taxes but also build a stronger, more profitable and resilient business in India.

Thank you for trusting me to guide you on this journey. Let's be smart and thrive together.

With gratitude,

CA Manish Gupta

❑ ❑ ❑

REAL TAX STORIES OF FOUNDERS

How Three Founders Smartly Saved Taxes in India

Starting a business in India as a foreign entrepreneur or NRI is exciting. There's energy in the air, a growing market to tap into, and endless opportunities. But you know what's not so exciting? Getting slapped with heavy taxes — the kind that could have been easily avoided with the right guidance. Over the years, I've seen founders lose *millions of dollars* not because they failed to build great businesses, but because they were unaware of basic tax-saving strategies that were well within their reach.

Let me tell you the stories of three founders — Alex from the USA, Soo-Jin from Korea, and James from the UK. Each of them began their India journey with big dreams... but were in for some big surprises when it came to taxes. Thankfully, they discovered a few smart strategies (yes, the same ones we'll cover in this book), and everything changed.

1. Alex from the USA: "Wait... I Have to Pay 20% Just to Send Money Back?"

Alex, a tech founder from the U.S., had set up a company in India. Business was booming — Indian operations were profitable, and he was ready to repatriate some of that money back to his main company in the States.

Then he got the news:

"20% TDS (withholding tax) will be deducted."

Alex nearly choked on his coffee. "Twenty percent? Just like that? That's huge!"

At first, he assumed that's just how Indian tax worked. He didn't want to argue — so he paid. That's when we connected. We showed him one powerful strategy — one that's explained in the bonus chapter of this book.

Not only did he save over a million dollars in taxes... he also claimed credit for it in the U.S, bringing massive relief to his Finances.

2. Soo-Jin from Korea: "This GST... Can I Get It Back?"

Soo-Jin ran a sharp software company out of Bangalore. She had a lean, efficient team working from a co-working space, using paid tools and cloud services. One day, during a routine expense check, she noticed how much GST she was paying — 18% on almost everything: rent, software, consultants.

She assumed — like many foreign founders — that GST was just another cost of doing business in India.

When we reviewed her setup, we asked:

"Why aren't you claiming your GST input credit?"

Her response: *"Can I do that? Even if my company is foreign-owned?"*

Absolutely yes — if your business is structured right, registered properly, and filing the correct returns. That's what we helped her do. Over the next few months, Soo-Jin started reclaiming millions in GST she thought was lost.

The result? More working capital, better margins, and peace of mind.

3. James from the UK: "We Withheld 20% — That's Just How It Works, Right?"

James had set up a wholly owned subsidiary company in India. Things were going well — until they started paying overseas consultants from their Indian entity.

Like most companies, they were deducting 20% TDS on those

payments and depositing it with the Indian government. The twist? Their contracts said *"all taxes to be borne by the Indian company."* That meant they were paying the consultants plus taxes on top.

Millions were being paid unnecessarily — simply because they didn't know the alternatives.

When we stepped in, we used DTAA and helped them bring the TDS down to 0% — legally and cleanly.

Sure, the taxes already paid were gone. But **the future savings? Massive.**

One change in paperwork led to lakhs saved every month. It's not about cutting corners; it's about knowing where they are.

Why These Stories Matter

These three founders had different businesses, different countries, and different challenges. But they had one thing in common — **they were unknowingly overpaying taxes in India.** Once they learned the right strategies, everything changed.

And here's the good news:

These strategies aren't loopholes or hacks. They're **legitimate, law-backed tax-saving options** available under Indian law — but only if you know how to use them.

In the coming chapters, I'll walk you through these exact strategies — in plain English, with real-world context — so you can avoid the mistakes they almost made.

Because if you're going to do business in India...

You might as well do it smartly.

❑ ❑ ❑

What This Book Will Do for You

This book is your shortcut to legally saving taxes, avoiding costly mistakes, and building a compliant, stress-free business in India — without needing to become a tax expert.

You'll discover exactly where you may be unknowingly overpaying, learn step-by-step strategies that are simple to apply, and use ethical, risk-free methods already proven by successful NRI and foreign-owned businesses.

Backed by real-world insights, practical case studies, and simplified guidance, this book shows you how to save more, stay compliant, and scale with confidence — without the fear of tax notices, penalties, or regulatory shocks.

Whether you're just starting or already operating in India, this book gives you a powerful edge: peace of mind and profit protection, from day one.

Why You're Smart to Read This

Avoid the Overpayment Traps Before It's Too Late

If you're a foreign business owner or NRI planning to operate in India, this book may be one of the **smartest and most profitable investments** you make. Here's why reading this now can save you years of pain later:

1. Prevent Expensive Mistakes Before They Happen

Most foreign founders only realize their tax planning mistakes after years of overpayment, penalties, and exhausting back-and-forth with tax authorities. You'll learn these lessons before making the same costly errors.

2. Stop Wasting Time, Energy, and Money

Many entrepreneurs overpay taxes and then spend months trying to claim refunds. This book helps you avoid that entire cycle—saving you time, stress, and cash.

3. Learn in Hours What Others Learn in 10 Years

While most foreign entrepreneurs gain this knowledge through hard, costly experience, you'll get it all upfront—just by reading this book.

4. Step Ahead of the Curve

Simply by reading this, you'll be a step ahead of other NRI and foreign-owned businesses in India. You'll understand the tax nuances they wish they knew when they started and use them to your advantage from Day One.

5. Avoid the Tax Trap That Eats Into Your Profits

In India, taxes can take up 15% to 35% of your earnings—sometimes more than your actual profit margin. Smart business owners focus not just on growth, but also on optimizing their tax liabilities.

6. Plan Proactively Instead of Paying Reactively

This book shows you how smart tax planning done early can eliminate the last-minute stress, confusion, and financial strain of unexpected tax payments.

❑ ❑ ❑

WHO THIS BOOK IS FOR AND WHY YOU'LL THANK YOURSELF LATER

This book is your tax-saving survival guide. If you're dealing with India in any part of your business — directly or indirectly — this book was written with you in mind. Here's who it's tailored for:

Foreign Business Owners & NRIs Operating in India

Whether you're from the USA, UK, Korea, UAE, Germany, Singapore, Denmark or any other part of this lovely planet—if you're earning in India and losing sleep (or profits) over taxes, this book is your caffeine-free wake-up call.

Founders & Decision-Makers

CEOs, founders, or owners—whether you're already in India or planning to step in—this is for those who like to save millions of dollars instead of overpaying to the tax department unintentionally. Because good intentions don't reduce tax outflows. Smart decisions do.

Finance & Accounts Teams (India & Global)

For the folks deep in spreadsheets, reconciling numbers and wondering, "Are we really optimizing taxes?"—here's your answer key. Especially valuable for cross-border coordination and sanity checks.

Companies at Any Stage of Their Indian Journey

Whether you've just started operations or are planning to enter India or running company already in India, this book is your-warning system—it helps you avoid common mistakes, understand what taxes you should be paying (and what you shouldn't), and skip the trial-and-error phase, giving you clarity, confidence, and protection from the infamous 'surprise tax bill' syndrome.

You Know Who You Are

If you've ever heard the words "Don't worry, it's all taken care of" — and still feel unsure — this book is written for you.

It's for those who ask the hard questions, seek clarity and want real answers that go beyond surface-level advice.

If any part of your business touches India, even remotely, this book isn't just helpful — it's essential.

❑ ❑ ❑

Know Your Author

CA Manish Gupta | India Entry Strategist | International Tax Consultant | Author

CA Manish Gupta is a **first-generation entrepreneur** and the **founder of Manish Anil Gupta & Co. (MAG)**—a firm trusted by over 300 global businesses for managing their India tax and compliance matters. With more than **10 years of experience in international taxation and India entry strategies,** Manish has become the go-to advisor for foreign business owners and NRIs looking to operate smoothly and profitably in India.

He has advised clients from **15+ countries** across **50+ industries,** helping them set up, scale, and most importantly—**stop overpaying taxes in India.** His practical and result-driven approach has helped clients reclaim control over their compliances, reduce unnecessary tax outflows, and operate with greater confidence and peace of mind.

Manish is the **author of two insightful books:**

- "Hassle-Free Business Setup in India"
- "Stop Overpaying Taxes in India"

A **qualified Chartered Accountant,** his journey began when he personally spoke with over 300 foreign business owners. One common frustration echoed among them:

"We're overpaying taxes in India... and there's no clear strategy to fix it."

What he discovered was a widespread gap in the market—most consultants focused only on filing returns and submitting reports, while no **one was offering real tax-saving strategies** or clarity on planning. These entrepreneurs were often left in the dark, paying excessive taxes they could never recover, with no roadmap or guidance.

That frustration became his mission.

Today, Manish is leading the movement to simplify Indian tax laws for global businesses. He and his team focus not just on compliance, but on **ethical tax optimization**—offering a rare blend of clarity, strategy, and practical action to help foreign businesses thrive in India.

❑ ❑ ❑

Don't Be the Foreign Business Owner Who Overpays Taxes

Every year, thousands of foreign business owners enter the Indian market full of ambition—but unknowingly end up **paying far more in taxes than they need to.**

Why does this happen?

1. Because they never understood the Indian tax ecosystem.

Most foreign entrepreneurs dive in without a clear picture of how Indian taxes really work—missing out on legitimate tax benefits, exemptions, and opportunities for optimization that could save them millions.

2. Because they realized the mistakes too late.

It often takes years to discover they've been overpaying, and by then, there's little scope for correction or recovery.

3. Because they assumed their consultants were "taking care of it."

There's a common and dangerous misconception that as long as tax returns are filed on time, everything is under control. But most consultants focus only on compliance and reporting, not on proactive, strategic tax planning that can unlock huge savings.

4. Because they feared that planning meant inviting risk or scrutiny.

Many believe that any form of tax planning will lead to government audits or legal trouble. The truth is quite the opposite. **There are**

ethical, government-backed ways to reduce your tax burden. You just need to know where to look and how to implement them properly.

5. Because they believed they had to become tax experts themselves.

You don't need to master India's tax code or become your own advisor. But you do need the **right awareness**—enough to ask the right questions, make informed decisions, and work better with your consultants and advisors.

Don't be the business owner who realizes all this after years of financial loss.

Be the one who takes charge early, plans smartly, and builds a more profitable, compliant, and stress-free operation in India. This mindset not only protects your bottom line but also strengthens your business foundation for sustainable growth.

The difference between success and struggle in India often boils down to smart tax planning and that difference starts with you.

❑ ❑ ❑

The Hidden Tax Trap: Why Foreign Businesses Overpay in India and Losing 100 Million Every Year

Despite their best intentions and efforts, many foreign-owned businesses operating in India continue to **bleed profits through unnecessary and avoidable tax payments.** Why does this happen? Here are the most common reasons behind this costly trap:

1. Believing That Compliance Equals Optimization

Just submitting returns on government portals doesn't save you taxes. **Compliance is not the same as planning.** Without active strategies, you're very likely paying far more than required.

2. Assuming Tax Saving is Automatically Done by Your Consultant

While your consultant should be helping with tax planning, it is a mistake to assume they will do this automatically. As a business owner, you must initiate these critical conversations and demand clear explanations on how to legally minimize tax outflows. Don't leave savings on the table by being passive.

3. Lack of Execution Despite Having Information

You might know about possible tax-saving routes—but **without someone accountable to implement them,** the ideas remain on paper while tax liabilities pile up.

4. Choosing the Wrong Business Structure

A structure that doesn't align with your operations or goals can lead to **higher taxes, compliance burdens, or even double taxation.**

5. Not Leveraging the Double Taxation Avoidance Agreement (DTAA)

Many foreign companies fail to take full advantage of the DTAA benefits, leaving them open to **paying taxes both in India and their home country.** This costly mistake can be legally avoided by understanding and applying treaty provisions correctly.

6. Lack of In-House Planning and Oversight

Tax planning is often ignored at the organizational level, and with no internal accountability, **default payments become the norm—even when savings are possible.**

Don't fall into this trap. With the right awareness and planning, you can transform your tax burden into an opportunity for greater profit, compliance, and peace of mind.

❑ ❑ ❑

HOW INDIA TAXES FOREIGN BUSINESSES

If you're a foreign business owner or NRI planning to operate in India, it's crucial to understand which taxes apply to your company. This clarity is **the first step toward effective tax planning.** Let's break it down simply — no jargon, just the key facts you need to know.

1. Income Tax (Corporate Tax)

- **What it is:** Tax levied on the net profit of your business after all legitimate expenses.
- **How much:** Typically ranges between **15% to 35%,** depending on your business structure (e.g., Private Limited, LLP, Branch Office, Liaison Office, etc.).
- **Why it matters:** This is one of the largest tax components for your business. Strategic planning here can **save you millions of dollars every year** by legally optimizing your taxable income.

2. GST (Goods and Services Tax)

- **What it is:** An indirect tax on the sale and purchase of goods or services in India.
- **Rate:** GST rates vary from 0% to 28%, depending on the category of goods or services.
- **How it works:**
    - **When you sell goods or services:** You charge GST to your customer, which you then remit to the government.

- **When you purchase goods or services:** You pay GST, which can usually be claimed back as input tax credit, reducing your overall tax liability.

3. TDS (Tax Deducted at Source) - Withholding Taxes

- **What it is:** A tax deducted at the time of payment to suppliers, contractors, employees, or others.
- **When it applies:**
  - When making payments for services, rent, salaries, or any other specified expenses.
  - You, as the payer, are responsible for **deducting TDS** before releasing the payment and depositing it with the government.
  - For example, if you're paying a contractor, you'll need to deduct TDS before paying the invoice amount. Suppose you have to pay a contractor INR 1,00,000 with a 10% TDS rate: you pay them INR 90,000 and deposit INR 10,000 as tax.
- **Why it matters:** Non-compliance can lead to **penalties** and **interest charges.** Hence, it's essential to ensure timely and accurate deduction and payment of TDS.

4. Professional Tax

- **What it is:** A state-level tax applicable to employees and employers in certain states (around 16).
- **When it applies:** If you have an office or operations in any of these states, you must register and comply with professional tax regulations as per state laws.

5. ESI & PF (Social Security Contributions)

- **What it is:** Mandatory contributions towards employee welfare and social security benefits.
- **When applicable:** If you hire employees and their salaries fall under certain thresholds, you're required to contribute:
  - **PF (Provident Fund):** A retirement benefit scheme.
  - **ESI (Employee State Insurance):** Health insurance and social security for employees.

Smart Tax Planning Starts Here

Before making any tax-saving strategies, always begin with clear answers to these critical questions:

1. Which taxes are applicable to your specific business model and operations?

2. What legal structure is your company registered under in India?

3. What are your core business activities—selling goods, providing services, hiring staff, or all of these?

Once you have this clarity, **you can build a customized tax optimization plan** that keeps you compliant, efficient, and profitable in India.

❑ ❑ ❑

Chapter

01

How to Choose the Lowest Tax Rate in India: ETHICALLY!

"Tax is not the enemy; ignorance of it is."

When you're setting up a new company in India — whether as a foreign company or an NRI founder expanding your business — there are many priorities: business model, team building, product launch, and compliance.

But there's one silent factor that can quietly eat into your profits if ignored — **the corporate tax rate.**

Here's the Good News:

India allows you to choose your corporate tax rate. Yes, **you can legally opt for a lower tax rate** but only if you know the rule and act in time.

What Most Business Owners Don't Know

Every company registered in India, whether Indian-owned or foreign-owned, falls under the Indian corporate tax structure.

By default, companies are taxed at **22% or 30% (Excluding Surcharge and Cess),** depending on their turnover.

But here's the catch most founders don't know:

You can choose the lowest tax rate of **22% (excluding surcharge and cess)** simply by filing one form.

Sounds like a no-brainer, right?

But here's the twist:

- To enjoy this lower rate, you must file Form 10-IC — a one-time declaration.
- If you miss this filing, you'll automatically be taxed at the higher rate — even if you were eligible for the lower one.

How You Can Save Taxes in India

If you file **Form 10-IC** on time, you lock in the **22% base tax rate —**

- It's a one-time filing, but a lifetime of savings.
- No complicated paperwork, just strategic awareness.

What You Must Do – The Advisory Note

If you're a foreign business owner or NRI setting up in India, here's your simple tax-saving checklist:

- Don't assume you'll automatically get the lowest tax rate — **you must opt in.**
- **File Form 10-IC before filing your income tax return** to enjoy the 22% tax rate.
- Keep documentation ready in case of future assessments or audits.
- Consult your advisor but make sure you are in the driver's seat of this decision.

Final Thoughts

Choosing the right tax rate is not just about saving money; it's about laying the foundation for a **lean, profitable, and future-ready company.**

The 22% rate is yours for the taking but only if you act before it's too late.

❑ ❑ ❑

Chapter

02

Choose the Right Business Structure: Save Up to 13% in Taxes

"A mistake in structure today can echo in audit rooms tomorrow."

When you're starting a business in India as a foreign company or NRI, the first big decision is **how to structure it.**

Why? Because the right business structure can save you **up to 13% in taxes every year** and help you grow faster. In today's tight-margin environment, that kind of saving improves not just profits but your ability to reinvest, expand, and sustain.

This is why leading MNCs invest in proper tax structuring not to avoid tax, but to manage it efficiently. **It's ethical. It's strategic. And it's smart business.**

Let's decode the available options with clarity — and understand why choosing the right one is critical for doing business in India.

Why Structure Matters

Your business structure decides:

- How much tax you'll pay
- How easily you can raise funds or bring in investors

- How scalable and flexible your business will be — including exit planning

A wrong choice may lead to:

- Higher tax rate
- Unwanted legal restrictions
- Difficulty attracting investors

The 3 Main Structures for Foreign Companies in India

1. Private Limited Company - Best for Most Business

- Tax Rate: **22%**
- Ideal for active operations, product sales, tech services, BPOs, or startups.
- Offers limited liability, ease in raising capital, and access to government incentives.

2. LLP (Limited Liability Partnership) - Simple and Low Maintenance

- Tax Rate: **30%**
- Best for consulting or service-based models with fewer compliance needs.
- Not preferred if you're planning to raise investment from venture capital firms.

3. Branch or Liaison Office - For Representation Only

- Tax Rate: **35%**
- Used mainly to establish presence or explore market potential.
- Cannot engage in revenue-generating activities and has tighter RBI control.

What You Should Do

- If you're doing real business in India — like setting up back-end operations, hiring, selling products, or growing long-term — a **Private Limited Company** is usually the best choice.
- If you want a small, low-maintenance structure without investors, **LLP may suit you.**
- If you're still testing the Indian market and just want a physical presence, a **Branch or Liaison** Office works but keep in mind the high tax and limited scope.

Choosing the right structure is about aligning with your business goals. Many foreign founders wrongly assume all structures are taxed equally. That's a costly mistake.

Real Example

John, an entrepreneur from the US, rushed to set up a **Branch Office** in India, thinking it was the quickest route. He didn't realize the **35% tax rate** that came with it. Six months in, he was overwhelmed.

When he reached out to me, I advised him to **shut down the Branch Office and switch to a Private Limited Company.**

Within just 3 months:

- His tax rate dropped to 22%
- He started claiming tax benefits in both countries
- And he saved **13% in taxes,** which he used to hire more staff and expand operations

One correction saved lakhs in the first year alone.

My Advice

Start Smart!

Choose your business structure with long-term goals in mind not short-term ease. A structure chosen in a hurry can cost you in taxes, compliance, and missed opportunities. But the right one sets the stage for smooth operations, investor trust, and sustainable growth.

❑ ❑ ❑

Chapter

03

How Markup Invoicing Can Save You Global Taxes

"A good business earns. A better one knows when to pause and plan."

"**Manish,** we're just sending money to our Indian team as an advance to cover salaries — we're not raising any invoices from India, so we don't need to pay taxes in India because we don't have any revenue. That's okay, right?"

I've heard this line countless times from foreign founders, especially those running cost centers in India. And every time I hear it, I pause... because while it sounds harmless, it's actually a **tax trap waiting to explode.** The assumption is that since there's no customer or business in India, there's no need for invoicing—and hence, no tax liability.

But this can backfire — badly.

The Common Mistake

If your Indian entity receives money from your head office or parent company abroad—whether to pay salaries or meet expenses—you **must raise an invoice.** Not doing so is the first mistake.

Secondly, even if it's an advance, Indian regulations require you to **adjust that advance within 12** months by raising an invoice. If you don't, it becomes taxable in India.

It's a simple misunderstanding that can lead to **regulatory violations** and significantly increase your **global tax burden.**

What Actually Happens If You Skip Invoicing?

Let's understand with an example: your company sends money to the Indian entity as an advance. You use it to pay your team and run operations—but you don't raise any invoice with a markup.

Here's what can go wrong:

- When you receive advance payments and use them to pay salaries but do not raise invoices (i.e., show revenue with a markup), the **Indian tax department may later treat the advances as taxable income.**
- **In India:** You'll be asked to pay tax, interest, and possibly penalties—because there's no revenue invoice raised to match the expenses.
- **In the USA (or your home country):** Since there's no invoice from India, your company **can't claim the Indian salary costs as expenses.** As a result, your US company shows **inflated profits** and ends up paying more tax!

This is how you get **taxed twice**—once in India and again in your home country. Without realizing it, you've lost a **big chunk of your hard-earned profit.**

The Simple (and Smart) Fix: Markup Invoicing

The solution is surprisingly simple—**raise a regular invoice with a reasonable markup** to your parent company for the services provided from India.

Here's how this helps:

- The **Indian company shows legitimate revenue.**
- The **US company gets proper vendor bills**—and claims full expenses.
- **No interest or penalty worries.**
- You **avoid double taxation,** and everything stays **clean and compliant.**

What Should You Actually Do?

Here's your simple checklist:

- Raise invoices regularly from India to your parent company.
- Match your **advance received** with **invoices raised** within **12 months.**
- Keep documentation clear—especially **transfer pricing** and **service agreements.**

Bonus Tip: Keep a monthly review calendar. This ensures timely invoicing and helps you stay on top of compliance without last-minute panic.

Think Like a Global CFO

If you're operating across borders, don't think locally. You must think like a **Global CFO**—balancing **tax, compliance, and long-term visibility.**

Markup invoicing is not just an accounting task—it's a **tax-saving strategy.** One that's **simple, legal, and incredibly effective.**

Conclusion: Don't Let Laziness Cost You 22%

Skipping invoicing may feel like an administrative shortcut—but it's a dangerous one. In the long run, it can cost you more in **taxes, penalties, and audit risks.**

Raise those invoices. Add that markup. Keep your finances clean and save taxes in both India and your home country.

It's the easiest way to protect your profits globally and one of the smartest habits every founder should adopt early.

❑ ❑ ❑

Chapter

04

DTAA Secrets: Slash Your Tax by 100%

"An unplanned tax is a slow drain disguised as routine."

Let's say your Indian company wants to **send money to your parent company or a vendor overseas**—maybe for **royalties, support services, or even dividends.** Here's where many foreign founders get hit hard: **India deducts a flat 20% tax** before sending the money.

But what if you could **cut that tax down to 15%, 10% or even 0%?** Sounds too good to be true? It isn't and it's completely legal.

How can you achieve this? Let's discuss the strategy and its implementation before diving into the details of how it works in India.

Understanding the Basics:

If you are making payments to a **parent company or overseas vendors** for **royalties, support services** or technical consultancy, Indian regulations require you to **deduct withholding tax** and **deposit it with the Indian Government.** This withholding tax is typically **20% of the payment amount,** before the money even leaves India.

This creates a major challenge for business owners operating in India because a significant portion of their funds gets withheld by the government.

The Solution: Unlocking DTAA Benefits

To overcome this challenge, India offers a powerful (but often underutilized) tax-saving tool: the **Double Tax Avoidance Agreement (DTAA).**

Let's understand how it works and how it can dramatically reduce your tax burden, often **cutting it in half or more.**

What is DTAA?

DTAA stands for **Double Tax Avoidance Agreement.** It's a bilateral tax treaty that **India signs with other countries**—over **90 of them**, including the **USA, UK, Korea, Japan, UAE, and Singapore.**

The goal is simple:

- **To prevent the same income from being taxed twice** — once in India and once in your home country.
- **To Reduce withholding tax rates** in India based on the treaty.
- **To Improve your global cash flow** by lowering deductions.
- To offer **certainty and stability** to international businesses operating in India.

Real-World Example:

A Bengaluru-based startup, **NovaTech,** was regularly paying its **US-based IT vendor, TechPulse,** for routine IT services.

Following the default rule, their accountant, Sanjay, deducted **20% tax** before sending the money—as per Indian law. It was draining their budget. Every month.

Then came the turning point.

After a discussion with me, they found out that the **India-USA DTAA** allowed them to reduce the tax to **just 0%.**

Why?

Because they qualified for lower rate under DTAA, provided they submitted two simple documents:

1. **Form 10F**
2. **Tax Residency Certificate (TRC)**
3. **No PE Declaration**

They submitted these documents, claimed the **DTAA benefit,** and **stopped overpaying.**

That year alone, NovaTech saved over **₹20 lakhs**—money that went straight into growing their business.

Many Miss Out — Don't Be One of Them

Here's the truth: **many foreign business owners operating in India never use DTAA.** And that's **money left on the table, every single transaction.**

So whether you're paying your **parent company, a foreign consultant, or a vendor overseas—check if there's a DTAA between India and that country.** If there is, you could be eligible for **massive tax savings,** with just a bit of paperwork.

Advisory Note: Don't Just Deduct — Plan

Before making cross-border payments, **always seek proper advice** to ensure:

- You are **applying the correct article** under the applicable DTAA treaty.

- You have the required **documentation,** including:
    - **Tax Residency Certificate (TRC)** from the payee's home country
    - **Form 10F**
    - **No PE Declaration**

The **right strategy** can help you **save lakhs every year—legally and ethically.**

Conclusion: Stop Overpaying, Start Optimizing

In international business, knowledge isn't just power; it's **profit.**

If your accountant or advisor hasn't spoken to you about DTAA yet, it's time to have that conversation.

Claim what's legally yours. Submit what's needed. And slash that 20% tax rate, forever.

Your bottom line will thank you.

❑ ❑ ❑

Chapter

05

Optimize Your GST: Don't Let 18% Burn Your Budget

"Not all losses appear in red ink – some hide in missed claims and wrong methods."

GST in India is like that **silent expense** that sneaks up on you. If you're not careful, it can quietly **burn through your profits.** And honestly, many **foreign business owners and NRIs** don't even realize how much they're overpaying because of it.

You're **invoicing customers, buying services, renting office space,** and suddenly, that **0% to 28% GST is everywhere. In the industry,** an 18% GST is applied to most goods and services bought or sold in India. It's not a small cost; it can significantly **eat into your margins.**

But here's the good news—**there are smart ways to save on that 18% and even get it back!**

Let's talk about **two major strategies** to **cut your GST costs** in India.

Way 1: Get Rid of GST When You Export Services

Let's say you're offering **services from India to a foreign company**—like **marketing, consulting, technical support,** or even **reimbursements from your parent company for employee expenses.** Typically, GST is charged at **18%,** but if your services qualify as an **export of services,** you **don't need to charge GST at all.**

How Does That Work?

It's simple. You just need to **apply for a Letter of Undertaking (LUT)** with the Indian GST department. This small but powerful document is your **ticket to zero GST** on your invoices.

Here's what it does:

- **No GST on your bills** — you don't have to pay that 18%.
- **No upfront payments** that block your cash flow.
- **No need to go through the hassle of claiming refunds later.**

And the best part?

This is **100% legal and even encouraged by the government.** If you're exporting services, they **want you to do it without barriers.**

Way 2: Claim Back GST When You Pay for Services in India

Now, let's **flip the coin.**

Suppose you're purchasing services in India—things like software subscriptions, co-working spaces, consultancy fees, or **office supplies.** As a business, you're paying **18% GST** on these services.

But here's where you get smart: **You can claim that 18% back!**

The Magic of Input Tax Credit (ITC)

This is called **Input Tax Credit (ITC).** It's basically the government's way of saying, *"If you've paid GST on your expenses, you can claim it back."*

Here's how to make it work:

- **Keep proper invoices:** make sure they are GST-compliant and well-documented.
- **File your GST returns on time:** this is non-negotiable.
- **Claim the refund:** and the GST department will **give it back to you.**

That **18%?** It's not a real cost if you do it right; it's just about **managing your cash flow wisely.**

But There's a Catch:

You **must claim the refund within 2 years of the payment.** If you miss that deadline, the money is gone for good.

Real-Life Example: How a Company Lost and Then Learned

Let me share a quick story. A **Singapore-based marketing company** set up operations in India. They paid **GST on office rent, Zoom subscriptions, and consultancy fees**—all standard expenses.

But here's the problem: **they didn't know about ITC refunds.** They just assumed that GST was just a regular business cost.

Two years later, when they finally learned about ITC, it was **too late.** All that money was **gone.** It couldn't be claimed anymore.

But that mistake taught them something valuable. Today, they **track all their GST invoices, file returns regularly,** and **claim refunds on time.**

The difference? They now **save lakhs of rupees every year**—money that goes straight into their growth and expansion.

Advisory Wrap-Up: Your GST Optimization Checklist

Here's your **simple checklist** to optimize your GST:

- **Apply for LUT** before you start exporting services — and remember to **renew it yearly.**
- **Keep all GST bills** if you're paying for services in India — every invoice counts.
- **Claim your GST refund within 2 years** from the end of the financial year in which the tax was paid

Final Thoughts

Taking care of your GST planning can make a massive difference to your cash flow and bottom line.

Whether you're exporting services or operating in India, being GST-smart is being business-smart.

Don't let **18% quietly eat away at your profits**—be proactive, and use these savings to **fuel your business growth in India.**

❑ ❑ ❑

Chapter

06

Transfer Pricing: India's Silent Tax Trap

"You don't need to evade the system — just understand it better than most."

Is Your India Office Costing You More Than It Should?

Imagine you're running your Indian operations smoothly—your team is growing, projects are flowing in, and you're happily reimbursing the Indian entity for all its costs from your parent company abroad. You think, "We're just covering expenses, so we're good."

Then one day, you get a fat envelope from the Indian tax authorities, and it's not a holiday greeting. It's a notice saying you owe taxes—big ones. You stare at the paper, wondering: ***How? I'm just paying for my own costs. Where's the income?***

This, my friend, is the invisible tax trap called **Transfer Pricing**—and if you're not careful, it can quietly drain your profits. Let's break this down, step by step, and I promise it'll be as clear as day.

What Exactly is Transfer Pricing?

Think of Transfer Pricing as the price tag you put on any transaction between your Indian company and your parent company (or any related entity abroad). It's like selling services or products to yourself—but here's the catch:

Indian tax authorities want you to charge **fair market value,** even if you're just covering costs.

Why? Because if you undercharge, India loses tax revenue. If you overcharge, your costs inflate, and you pay unnecessary taxes. It's a delicate game of balance.

Three Simple Steps to Avoid the Trap

1. Set the Right Markup — Don't Follow the Giants

One common mistake many business owners make is copying the markup rates of large MNCs. Big corporations often have significant brand value, large client bases, and market dominance—so they can justify high markups. But as a smaller player, if you set your markup too high, you might end up inflating your costs and overpaying taxes unnecessarily.

Pro Tip: Choose a markup that matches your business scale, not the big giants. Benchmark against companies of your size and nature.

2. Only Mark Up What Actually Adds Value

Not every cost needs a markup. Here's where you can be smart:

- Reimbursement expenses
- Cost Contribution Arrangement
- Capital Contribution

Adding a profit margin here just inflates your costs and your tax bill. Keep these pure and straightforward.

Pro Tip: Only mark up where value is actually being added—like tech development, marketing, or operational support.

3. Segment Your Activities Clearly

If your Indian entity handles multiple functions—like software development, marketing, and admin support—don't lump everything together. Different activities should be categorized separately. When you segment properly, it's easier to justify your markups and avoid unnecessary taxes.

Pro Tip: Segmenting these keeps your finances clean and reduces your tax burden.

Real-Life Insight: How AlphaTech Saved ($10,000)

AlphaTech, a Singapore-based tech firm, was running its Indian operations for development and support. Initially, they applied the same markup rate for both segments—development and admin support. This lumped-up approach made their costs look artificially inflated.

When we stepped in, we helped them segment their activities properly. Development services got a fair markup, while admin support, where minimal value is added, had no markup. The result? They saved ($10,000) in just one financial year—money that went back into growing their team and expanding their projects.

Wrap-Up: Make Transfer Pricing Work for You

Transfer Pricing isn't just a rule; it's a strategy. Get your markup right, segment your activities, and know where not to apply markups. These small shifts can save you lakhs every year and keep you off the taxman's radar.

❑ ❑ ❑

Case Study

01

How Daniel Saved $8,450 in Tax Just by Smart Segmentation

Client Background

Daniel is a US-based founder who set up his India operations to support his growing SaaS business. His Indian entity had two distinct service lines:

- **Software Development**
- **Digital Marketing & Support**

In FY 2024-25, the India team scaled to 80 employees with total operational costs of **$1.2 million.**

The Challenge

Daniel's accountant applied a **flat 15% markup** across all activities without differentiating between them.

This led to:

- **Declared Profit:** $1,200,000 × 15% = **$180,000**
- **Tax Paid:** $180,000 × 25.168% = **$45,300**

The flat approach **overstated profit** on functions like marketing support, which typically warrant a lower markup.

Our Strategy: Functional Segmentation with Accurate Markups

After reviewing internal cost allocations and global pricing benchmarks, we segmented the functions:

- $720,000 on Software Development → **15% markup**
- $480,000 on Marketing Support → **8% markup**

New Calculation After Segmentation

- Software: $720,000 × 15% = **$108,000 profit**
- Marketing: $480,000 × 8% = **$38,400 profit**
- Total Declared Profit: **$146,400**
- Tax Paid: $146,400 × 25.168% = **$36,850**

The Outcome

- **Tax Saved:** $8,450
- **Time to Implement:** 3 weeks
- **Cash Flow Benefit:** Immediate
- **Structure Used:** Function-wise Transfer Pricing Segmentation

Key Takeaway

Don't blindly apply a flat markup. If your India team handles varied services — tech, support, marketing — segment the costs, apply **industry-aligned markups,** and reduce excess tax exposure.

❑ ❑ ❑

Chapter

07

How PE Leads to Double Taxation

"You don't lose money only in markets — you lose it in missed deductions and avoidable errors."

Many foreign business owners expanding into India are shocked when they receive a **tax notice - this time from India - even after paying taxes in their home country.**

They think, *"But I have a subsidiary in India, we're compliant. How can India send us a tax demand?"*

Here's the truth:

You can still be taxed in India even if you already have a company here — if you're not careful about how your foreign company operates.

Let me break it down simply.

Here's What Typically Happens:

You've set up a proper Indian company — great.

But your **foreign company is also active in India in ways it shouldn't be.** This can trigger what's called a **Permanent Establishment (PE)** under Indian tax laws.

PE (Permanent Establishment) = A fixed place of business or recurring business activity that causes a foreign company to become taxable in India.

This typically includes:

- Your foreign company's employees perform services in India **for a period exceeding the specified threshold** (often 90 or 183 days, depending on the applicable tax treaty).
- A **dependent agent** in India habitually concludes contracts on behalf of the foreign company or secures orders almost exclusively for it.
- You **set up a small office, coworking space, or base of operations** under the foreign entity's name.
- You operate a **construction, installation, or assembly project,** or conduct **supervisory activities** in India lasting more than a prescribed period.

If any of this applies, the Indian tax department may classify your foreign company as having a **Permanent Establishment (PE)** in India.

Now, even though you're already paying tax in your home country, the Indian authorities say:

"Your foreign company is active here. It's running operations and earning profits in India. So, you owe taxes here too."

And boom — you receive a tax notice, often with interest and penalties.

Real Story – What Went Wrong for a Foreign Company

A German software company had an Indian subsidiary and thought everything was in order.

But here's what they overlooked:

- Their **headquarters kept sending employees to India** for long durations to assist with operations and client interactions.

A few months later, they were shocked to receive a **tax demand from Indian authorities.**

Why?

Because under Indian tax laws, **sending employees for extended periods** can mean your **foreign company is effectively operating inside India** — creating what's known as a **Permanent Establishment (PE).**

So even though they were already paying taxes in Germany, **India wanted its share too.**

Why? Because their foreign company was **"acting like a business" inside India,** even if unintentionally.

This came with **tax demands, interest, and penalties** all of which could have been avoided with the right planning.

What You Should Avoid Doing from Day One

To avoid surprise tax demands, **don't do these from your foreign company without proper structure:**

- **Sending your team to work in India long-term:** Cross the allowed number of days, and your company can trigger a Service PE — making it taxable in India.
- **Letting someone in India close deals for you:** If a sales rep or agent is habitually **finalizing contracts or securing orders,** it qualifies as a **Dependent Agent PE.**

Even if they're not on payroll, their actions can create tax exposure.

- **Opening an office or coworking desk under the foreign company's name:** Even a single desk or mailing address = **Fixed Place PE.** India sees it as business being done here.

- **Running a project or site for too long:** If your construction, installation, or project work in India exceeds **6 to 9 months,** it may trigger a **Construction PE.**

That means India can tax your foreign company on the income earned from that project.

If You Don't Have One Yet...

- **Register your foreign company properly in India** — whether as a liaison office, branch office, or project office.
- Or better yet, **channel business through your Indian company** with the right agreements and structures in place.

Because half-measures or informal setups often lead to costly tax consequences.

Simple Rule:

Either do business through your Indian company, or register your foreign company correctly.

But don't mix the two without understanding the tax impact.

Final Advice

Set it up right from the beginning — or it will cost you much more later.

Before you:

- Send your team to India
- Sign a deal with an Indian client
- Start a project from your HQ

...consult a professional.

Let's plan things correctly so your business grows freely, **without tax troubles** — in India or abroad.

❑ ❑ ❑

Bonus Chapter

Repatriate Profits from India Without Paying Double Tax

"Every tax saved legally is capital earned without risk."

Congratulations!

Your business in India is now profitable — and it's time to bring some of that hard-earned money back to your home country.

But here's where many smart entrepreneurs slip up... if you don't plan this step carefully, you could end up paying **tax twice** — once in India and again in your home country.

This is where most foreign entrepreneurs make costly mistakes.

The good news? With smart planning, you can **legally and efficiently repatriate profits without facing double taxation.**

Two Legal Ways to Repatriate Profits from India

When your Indian company earns profits and you want to move those funds to your holding company or personal account abroad, there are **two main legal methods:**

- **Dividends**
- **Buyback of Shares**
- **NO PE Declaration**

Both options are fully approved by Indian regulators and are commonly used by multinational companies operating in India.

What's the Real Problem?

When you repatriate money (either as dividends or buyback proceeds):

- India deducts **TDS (Tax Deducted at Source)** — often **up to 20%**
- Your **home country may again tax the same income**

Without proper planning, you're at risk of **paying tax in both countries** — meaning you give away a large part of your profits to taxes, instead of enjoying them back home.

How to Avoid Double Taxation

Yes, India charges TDS on repatriated income — usually **20%** by default.

But here's where smart structuring helps:

If your country has a **Double Taxation Avoidance Agreement (DTAA)** with India, **you can reduce this tax burden significantly.**

Countries like the **USA, UK, Singapore, UAE,** and many others have DTAA treaties with India.

Under DTAA:

- TDS on dividends or buybacks can be **reduced to 5%-15%.**
- You can claim **Foreign Tax Credit (FTC)** in your home country for the tax already paid in India

Also ensure you're claiming **the correct DTAA article** (Article 10 for dividends, Article 13 for capital gains, etc.) — mistakes here are common and can delay or deny tax credit abroad.

Example

Let's say your company repatriates **₹1 crore as dividend.**

- Under DTAA, India deducts **10% TDS,** so you receive **₹90 lakhs** in your overseas account.

- Later, while filing your tax return in your home country, you declare that **₹10 lakhs was already paid** as tax in India.
- That amount is **credited against your total tax liability,** so you don't pay tax again on the same income.

This is why **DTAA compliance + timely paperwork** is critical.

Plan Smart, Repatriate Smooth

Repatriating profits from India **isn't complicated** — but it does require clarity and compliance.

Stick to these basics:

- Use either **dividends** or **share buybacks**
- Apply the relevant **DTAA rate**
- **File Form 10F**
- **Obtain your Tax Residency Certificate**
- **Maintain proper documentation** of all remittances for smooth FTC claims
- **No PE Declaration**

Many companies delay repatriation, thinking it's better to pile profits. But this can create **cash trap risks,** regulatory red flags, or missed tax treaty benefits.

Do this right — and you'll enjoy your profits back home without giving a major share away to unnecessary taxes.

❑ ❑ ❑

Case Study

02

Cutting Dividend Tax from 20% to 5% Using DTAA

Mauritius Case Study

Client: Finovate India Pvt. Ltd.

Industry: Fintech & Digital Payments

Scenario: Dividend repatriation to a Mauritius-based parent company

The Challenge

Finovate India Pvt. Ltd. wanted to repatriate **$300,000** as dividends to its Mauritius-based parent company.

But under default Indian tax laws, this dividend payout would attract a **20% withholding tax** — meaning **$60,000** would be deducted and paid to the Indian government.

That's a significant cash loss to the foreign shareholder — almost one-fifth of the total profit distribution.

Most companies are unaware that **this rate is reduced under tax treaties.** They pay the full 20%, assuming it's mandatory.

This case was a perfect example of how understanding tax structures can create **direct financial impact.**

Our Strategy

We stepped in and reviewed the **India-Mauritius DTAA.**

As per **Article 10**, a **5% tax rate** applies on dividends if the foreign shareholder holds at least **10% of the Indian company's shares.**

Our client qualified — so we proceeded to apply this reduced rate legally.

Compliance Steps

To ensure proper benefit, we arranged and filed:

- Tax Residency Certificate (TRC) from the Mauritius parent company
- Form 10F - properly filled and signed by an authorized representative
- No PE Declaration (confirming no Permanent Establishment in India)
- Proper resolution and documentation of shareholding pattern

All documents were shared with the bank and attached to the remittance request.

The Outcome

- **TDS Paid:** $15,000 (instead of $60,000)
- **Tax Saved:** $45,000
- **Time Taken:** 5-7 working days
- **Cash Flow Benefit:** Immediate and substantial

Key Lesson

If you're paying dividends to a foreign shareholder in a DTAA country like the Mauritius — don't settle for the default 20% rate.

Get the documents right, apply the DTAA, and unlock major tax savings.

❑ ❑ ❑

Reviews That Matter

1. As an NRI setting up my first company in India, I had zero idea about tax structuring. This book made everything crystal clear — from DTAA to GST. If you're entering India, **read this before you spend a single rupee.**

Prof. Dr. Sc Elena Surovyatkina, ***Senior Scientist, Germany***

Monselena Elena Monsoon

Forecast (India) Private Limited

2. I'm not from a finance background, but this book spoke my language. Easy to follow, no complex terms and it helped me understand and apply major tax-saving strategies. Highly recommended!

Lubna Shaikh, ***Executive Head, USA***

McFarland Engineering Services Private Limited

3. The **real-life examples and 'mistakes to avoid'** were eye-openers. We changed our invoice process and claimed GST credits we were missing out. We even got a refund from the government.

Pablo Alvarado, ***Director, Coast Rica***

Revbiolife Sciences Private Limited

4. For any NRI or foreign business owner entering India — this is a shortcut to **10 years of tax insights.** No fluff, only what matters. We structured our India ops right from day one because of this.

Daniel Park, ***Founder, Korea***
Hitech Rail Infra Services Private Limited

5. We were using the wrong transfer pricing method — a costly mistake. We also learned to segment our services and apply lower margins where needed. This book helped us correct it, **reduce markup by 3%, and save several lakhs.** These structuring tips were truly game-changing.

Sandeep Baiwdan, ***Co-Founder, USA***
Powerminds Consultancy Private Limited

6. DTAA always felt complex, but this guide made it incredibly easy to understand. We applied the strategy and legally **cut our tax rate by 10%.**

Pradip Keshvala, ***Founder (India)***
Techdroid Media Private Limited

7. **"He Helped Us Save More Taxes"**

"We always aimed to stay compliant, but the real surprise was how Manish helped us identify gaps, plug risks, and streamline our entire finance operations — saving us a significant amount in taxes."

Suvrat, *Founder, USA*

Gan Studio Private Limited

8. ***"A Must-Read for Business Owners Entering India"***

I recently found a book written specifically for global founders expanding into India — and Stop Overpaying Taxes stands out. It's practical, clear, and filled with real examples that make tax and compliance easy to understand. A great guide for avoiding costly mistakes.

Muthu Solayappan, *Director, USA*

Plan Optimus Software Services Private Limited

9. ***"A Must-Read for Anyone Who Wants to Save Tax and Grow in India"***

This book is a one-stop solution for global founders. Every tax-saving and business strategy is clearly explained and easy to apply. If you're serious about growth in India, this is all you need.

Sunil Tripathy, *CEO, USA*

Kodeshash Technologies Private Limited

10. "Made Indian Tax Complexity Simple"

I initially thought India's tax system was too complex to navigate. But this book breaks it down with such simplicity that even non-finance founders can take confident action.

Balraj Sura, ***Director, UK***

Intransitive Tech Services Private Limited

❑ ❑ ❑

What to Do Next: I've Read the Strategies. Now what?

Let's talk honestly — just you and me.

You've come this far in the book, read the strategies, understood the mistakes most foreign businesses make in India... and now you're probably thinking:

"Okay, Manish, this all sounds great but what do I actually do next?"

At this point, you've got **two clear choices.**

Choice 1: Do It Yourself

You've got the knowledge.

The 7 tax-saving strategies I've shared — along with the bonus tip — are practical and doable.

You can take this info, gather your team, sit with your consultant, and start implementing them.

And honestly?

If you're committed, and if you have the time — **you can make it work.**

But here's where most business owners get stuck...

They get busy.

They delay.

They try to squeeze India tax planning into their already packed schedule.

And what happens?

Either they don't fully implement...

Or they make a mistake that ends up costing them **millions in back taxes, penalties, or wasted time.**

I've seen it happen again and again.

And let's face it — yo**ur core job is to grow your business,** hire your team, build partnerships, or scale your product. Tax strategy shouldn't eat up your bandwidth.

Even if you get it right, it might take **years** to get the real results — and that's time you could've used to grow faster.

Choice 2: Book a 1:1 Strategy Call — My Gift to You

Now just pause for a moment... and imagine this:

Instead of figuring all this out on your own — trying one thing, then another, not sure what's right — you and I sit down for a **private, one-on-one call.**

Just you and me.

In that call, we'll go deep into:

- How your business is structured for tax planning
- Which **2–3 of the 7 strategies** will actually work for **your specific business**
- Plus, from my **additional 21+ proven strategies,** I'll handpick the ones that can give you **fast, measurable tax savings** which I could not include due to limited space in the book.

I'll also tell you what **not** to waste time or money on — because let's be honest, **not every strategy fits every business.**

This is expert-level advice — the same way I've helped clients from the **US, UK, Korea, UAE, and 15+ other countries** for over a **decade,** saving **millions in taxes.**

I'll tell you what works. What doesn't. And what **you** should focus on right now.

Normally, I charge **$ 250** for this kind of 1:1 strategy session.

Why? Because it saves businesses **millions in the long run and creates real results.**

But since you've made the effort to read this book — and I know you're serious —

I want to **gift this session to you. No charge.**

But let me be upfront with you:

I run a firm. I manage a team. I work closely with foreign businesses — so my calendar is **tight.**

I only offer a **limited number of strategy calls** each month, and once the slots are gone — that's it.

So, if this sounds like something you want to grab — **don't wait.**

How to Claim Your Free 1:1 Strategy Call:

Email: info@manishanilgupta.com

WhatsApp: +91 81305 61754

Use the code: "Book Reader 1:1 Gift" in your message.

Final Thought

You've got two options:

1. Keep figuring this out on your own. It might work — but it could take you **3 to 5 years** to get the results you want.

2. Or fast-track your journey with someone who's helped **300+ foreign businesses** set up and scale in India, saving **millions of dollars in taxes.**

The choice is yours.

~CA Manish Gupta

❑ ❑ ❑